How Do Engineers Solve Problems?

 HOUGHTON MIFFLIN HARCOURT

PHOTOGRAPHY CREDITS: 3 (b) ©JCVSTOCK-ES\Fotolia; 4 (b) Comstock/Getty Images; 8 (t) Stockbyte/Getty Images; 9 (l) ©JGI/Jamie Grill/Getty Images; 9 (r) Image100/Alamy; 10 (t) Comstock / Getty Images; 10 (bl) ©Corbis; 10 (r) ©Reven T.C. Wurman/Alamy Images; 10 (tr) ©Scanrail/Fotolia; 10 (cr) Jupiterimages/Getty Images

Printed in China

ISBN: 978-0-544-07219-0

15 16 17 18 0940 20 19 18 17

4500693646   A B C D E F G

Be an Active Reader!

 Look at these words.

engineer	human-made
design process	natural
materials	

 Look for answers to these questions.

What does an engineer do?

What is the design process?

How can we solve a problem?

What are objects made of?

How can we classify materials?

What does an engineer do?

An engineer finds answers to problems. Engineers make plans. Plans show how to make things. Engineers plan how to build machines. Engineers make machines safe.

Engineers build houses. They build bridges. They build ships, too.

Engineers make plans to build planes.

What is the design process?

The design process is a set of steps. Engineers follow steps to solve problems.

1. Find a Problem
2. Plan and Build
3. Test and Improve
4. Redesign
5. Communicate

This plan shows how to make a building.

How can you solve this problem?

This is one way to solve the problem. What is another way to solve it?

Here is a problem: You don't have a place for your pencils and markers. You build a pencil holder. How can you see if it works? How can you make your pencil holder better?

How can you solve this problem?

How can we solve a problem?

You can solve a problem. Follow five steps.

1. Find a Problem: A plant gets too much sun.

2. Plan and Build: Think of a way to solve the problem. Draw pictures of your plan. You build a shade. The shade can be put over the plant.

3. Test and Improve: The plant shade falls down. You find out it needs to be smaller.

4. Redesign: Build the shade smaller. Now you try the shade again. It works!

5. Communicate: Tell a friend about your plan. Show how you made it.

Sharing your plan helps a friend.

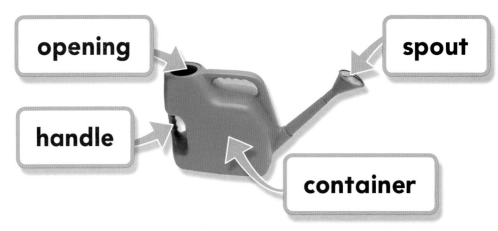

opening

spout

handle

container

What are objects made of?

Many objects have parts. The parts work together to make an object work.

Objects are made of materials. A watering can may be plastic or metal. How does a watering can help you?

- Pour water into the opening. The watering can holds water.
- Lift the watering can by its handle.
- Now water a plant!

> **Wool comes from sheep. It can be made into mittens.**

> **Bottles and cans are made by people.**

Human-made materials are made by people. A plastic bottle is human-made. You can wash it and use it again! It can also be made into another object.

Natural materials are found in nature. Wood in some desks comes from trees.

How can we classify materials?

Look at the objects below. Name each one. Tell whether the object is made from natural or human-made materials. Is it made of both?

Draw the chart below in your science notebook. Classify, or sort, the objects from page 10. Draw each object in the correct column. Label each object.

Sort the Objects

Natural	Human-made	Both

Draw and Label

Fold a sheet of paper in half. Draw something natural on the left. Draw something human-made on the right. Label both. Show them to a partner. Answer questions about each object: *What is its shape? How big or small is it? How does it feel?*

 ## Plan, Build, and Test

Make a plan to keep your desk neater. Write and draw your plan on paper. Build and test your design. Make it better. Share your design with a classmate.